MARIANNE NORTH
AT KEW GARDENS

Waterlily, *Nymphaea capensis* var *capensis*, and surrounding vegetation in Van Staadens Kloof.
The orchid is *Disa tripetaloides;* behind are various species of *Zamia, Euphorbia,*
Aloe and *Agapanthus.*

MARIANNE NORTH
· AT KEW GARDENS ·

LAURA PONSONBY

Published in association with the Royal Botanic Gardens, Kew

Webb & Bower

First published in Great Britain in 1990 by
Webb & Bower (Publishers) Limited,
5 Cathedral Close, Exeter, Devon EX1 1EZ
in association with the Royal Botanic Gardens, Kew

Distributed by the Penguin Group
Penguin Books Ltd, Registered Offices: Harmondsworth, Middlesex, England
Penguin Books Australia Ltd, Ringwood, Victoria, Australia
Penguin Books Canada Ltd, 2801 John Street, Markham, Ontario, Canada L3R 1B4
Penguin Books (NZ) Ltd, 182-190 Wairau Road, Auckland 10, New Zealand

Designed by Peter Wrigley

Text and Illustrations © Board of Trustees of the Royal Botanic Gardens, Kew, 1990

British Library Cataloguing in Publication Data

Marianne North at Kew Gardens, 1830-1890
1. Paintings. Special Subjects
I. North, Marianne, 1830-1890 –
758′5

ISBN 0–86350–309–8

Text is set in Janson Text 55

Typeset in Great Britain by P&M Typesetting Ltd, Exeter, Devon

Colour and mono reproduction by Mandarin Offset, Hong Kong

Printed and bound in Hong Kong

CONTENTS

PREFACE

The Marianne North Gallery has been one of the greatest treasures of Kew since it first opened in 1882 and it has continued to delight the often unsuspecting visitors who have made their way to this Victorian building in a lesser-known area of the Gardens near the Temperate House.

Eight hundred and thirty-two close-packed botanical paintings, nearly all painted in the wild, from many countries of the world, are displayed in a gallery designed under Miss North's supervision. The architecture is curious and includes features of Greek temple design, hand-painted surrounds to the doors, and the lower parts of the walls clad in 246 different types of wood which the artist collected during her travels. But one hardly notices the architecture. The sheer impact of the richly coloured oil paintings, frequently executed under conditions of extreme discomfort and in hazardous places, overwhelms the viewer and always prompts the question: 'Who was this extraordinary woman?'

The tale of her life and travels has been told in her two-volume autobiography *Recollections of a Happy Life*, and a third volume *Further Recollections of a Happy Life* was put together after Miss North's death by her sister Catherine Symonds. These books are rare and require concentrated reading as they have only a few black-and-white photographs and maps to enliven the text.

The publication in 1980 by Webb and Bower with the Royal Botanic Gardens, Kew, of *A Vision of Eden*, which contains a shortened and edited version of *Recollections* and beautiful reproductions of many of her paintings, first brought Marianne North to the attention of a wider public.

1990 is the centenary of the death of this outstanding Victorian lady traveller and, once again, Webb and Bower together with Kew has produced a collection of Marianne North's finest paintings, many of which have never previously been published.

They asked Laura Ponsonby, the great authority on her life and work, to write a concise biography, drawing on unpublished material in the archives at Kew and elsewhere. Miss Ponsonby has also contributed detailed captions to the paintings which highlight the importance of the plants and the scenes depicted, many of which are now under threat from the activities of mankind and some of which have gone for ever.

I welcome this beautiful book and am sure that, one hundred years after her death, it will elevate Marianne North to her rightful position among the great plant explorers of the Victorian age.

Professor G T Prance
Director
Royal Botanic Gardens, Kew

OPPOSITE: Foliage, pitchers and flowers of the carnivorous Bornean pitcher plant, *Nepenthes mirabilis*, with the orchid, *Papilionanthe hookeriana*, Sarawak.

The moon reflected in a turtle pool with a view of St Anne's Island from Marianne's
window at Mahé, Seychelles, with a coconut palm in the foreground.

INTRODUCTION

Shrewsbury station is not perhaps a place where many people sit and write letters, but it was there, on 11 August 1879, that Marianne North took up her pen to write to Sir Joseph Hooker, the Director of the Royal Botanic Gardens, Kew, to enquire whether he would accept her paintings as a gift to Kew. Marianne North had missed her train and, characteristically, not wishing to be idle even for an hour or two, wrote her letter, putting forward an idea which she had been brooding over for some time. It had in fact been suggested after her exhibition in Conduit Street earlier that year that the paintings should find their ultimate home at Kew.

In her letter to Sir Joseph, Marianne not only proposed to build a gallery to house the pictures, which would have a guardian's house and studio attached, but wanted visitors to be provided with 'tea or coffee and biscuits (nothing else)... at a fair price'. Sir Joseph acquiesced in all but the refreshments, which at that time were not allowed in the gardens, and pointed out in any case the impossibility of keeping the Great British Public in order, especially on a Bank Holiday, when there might be 77,000 people all at once.

Marianne North asked her friend, James Fergusson (1808–1886), the architectural historian and author of *A History of Architecture*, to design the building, and she herself chose the site, which was to be well away from the Main Gate and all the fashionable promenaders. It would be found only by those who really cared for plants and had taken the trouble to make their way through all the greenhouses. They would be rewarded with portraits of many of the plants they had just seen, pictured in their native habitats, and would have a place to rest and shelter from the elements if needed.

Even today the Gallery is found by comparatively few visitors. The weary and thirsty, having got thus far, are enticed by the promise of refreshments, now available nearby, and barely give the North Gallery a second glance. Those who unwittingly do decide to ascend the steps are totally unprepared for the sight which meets their eyes, and their look of utter astonishment and bewilderment is worth beholding. Before them and around them are tier upon tier of brightly coloured paintings of plants, landscapes, birds, animals and insects. Wilfrid Blunt (1901–1988), author and artist, once compared them to postage stamps stuck closely together in a gigantic botanical postage-stamp album. In 1882, while Marianne was busy arranging her pictures in the Gallery, a man pushed his way in and commented rudely, 'It isn't true about these all being painted by one woman is it?' When told it was Marianne herself who had done them all, he clasped her by both hands and declared, 'You! then it is lucky for you that you did not live two hundred years ago or you would have burnt for a witch'. Today visitors are equally astonished to hear that the 832 paintings in the Gallery were completed by one woman in thirteen years of travel around the world. Then the questions begin – when did Marianne North live? Where did she learn to paint? How did she travel? or, simply, Who was she?

Marianne North aged twenty-four: a portrait by Sir William John Newton (1785–1869) at Rougham.

EARLY YEARS

Marianne North was the daughter of Frederick North MP (1800–1869) and was born in Hastings on 24 October 1830. Her mother was the eldest daughter of Sir John Marjoribanks, Member of Parliament for Berwickshire, and widow of Robert Shuttleworth of Gawthorpe Hall in Lancashire. Marianne's mother was extremely ill before her birth and by 23 October Mr North had virtually given up any hope of the child being born alive. However by the 24th he happily reported to his diary that there was 'a girl in the world' and by the 25th he recorded that she was already being referred to as 'Miss North'. The North family home was at Rougham in Norfolk, but family quarrels resulted in Marianne's great-grandfather and grandfather living in Hastings. The Norths were descendants of the famous Roger North (1653–1734), lawyer, historian, musician and author of the lives of his three distinguished brothers. Frederick North built Hastings Lodge, where Marianne was born, but also lived in the family house from time to time. Marianne had a half-sister, Janet, who was many years older, a brother, Charles, two years her senior, and a sister, Catherine, seven years younger. Marianne was always known to her family and friends as 'Pop'; even today the North family talk affectionately of 'Aunt Pop' and her Gallery at Kew.

There was much journeying about in Marianne's childhood; the winters were usually spent in Hastings, the spring in London and the summer between Rougham and Gawthorpe Hall. The North family had a succession of governesses, but Marianne said they hardly interfered with her and she learnt all her history and geography from reading Scott, Shakespeare and Robinson Crusoe.

At one point it was decided that Marianne was totally uneducated and so she was sent to school in Norfolk. She found it hateful and all the girls, except one, uninteresting.

Like many well-to-do families of those days, the North family travelled around Europe; extended visits coincided with the periods when Mr North had failed to get into Parliament. Elected to Parliament as a Liberal in the year of Marianne's birth, by ten freemen of the town of Hastings (one of whom was himself!), he was forced to resign from ill-health two years later. He became an MP again from 1854 to1865 and was re-elected in 1868, only to be implicated in a bribery scandal, which greatly affected his already failing health.

It was in 1847 when Marianne was nearly seventeen that the North family, with the exception of her half-sister who had married the educationalist, Robert Kay, and her brother, took off for Heidelberg, where they stayed for eight months. They were accompanied by three maids, a German cook and an elderly English governess, who it was said knew the entire peerage by heart but whom Marianne hated. This was followed by two years travelling around Europe, renting houses or apartments and sometimes getting caught up in riots (1848 was the year of revolutions in Europe); in Vienna they escaped with their luggage in two wheelbarrows and in Dresden a revolution started the day after their arrival.

At this period music was Marianne's mania and a great deal of the time was spent having music lessons, practising and going to concerts. She had a beautiful singing voice, and in Dresden it was

Cork trees, *Quercus suber*, in Lisbon in Da Castro's garden, where the first
orange tree in Europe was said to be planted. Marianne made many trips to
Europe, especially with her family when young.

discovered that it was contralto not soprano. Marianne sometimes spent eight hours a day singing and playing the piano. In Brussels she admitted that her practising was more incessant than ever and probably a perfect nuisance to the neighbours and she wished it could be done silently. Mr North did not care for music and thought it 'a horrid noise which must be submitted to for the sake of others who like it'. Eventually the family returned to England and the passion for music continued, with lessons from Madame Sainton Dolby, the well-known singer, whom Marianne admired enormously. Madame Dolby made Marianne perform solo parts in some of her concerts, but uncontrollable nervousness always marred the occasion. Marianne's sister, Catherine, believed that singing was where her real genius lay, but sadly the beautiful voice

deserted her just when its cultivation reached its highest point.

Life at Rougham continued, with Marianne enjoying riding, singing and painting, but preferring to keep away from social events – balls to her were a penance. She hated dressing up and loathed the perpetual dreary talk of her partners and the general formality of the occasions. She preferred to be out on her donkey or pony being dragged under some hedge or across fields, events which were to serve her well in later life.

At Hastings there were many musical evenings, where both amateur and professional musicians performed. Sometimes zeal was greater than skill and on one memorable occasion Romberg's Toy Symphony was played, by a distinguished cast which included Prosper Sainton on the violin and his wife Madame Dolby playing the big drum 'with a will'. Marianne remembered Agnes Zimmermann, aged eight, perched on a high stool, playing Beethoven sonatas. One wonders how Mr North endured the music, but his increasing deafness no doubt protected him from over-zealous performances and the sound of the big drum! Mrs North was said to care neither for music nor art.

Marianne's mother died in 1855, the year after Mr North had been re-elected to Parliament. She had been in ill-health for some years, and before she died made Marianne promise never to leave her father. Hastings Lodge was let and Mr North and the girls took a flat in London. During the summer periods, when the House was not sitting, Mr North and his daughters would tour the Continent; as usual they met many celebrities including the scientist Professor Tyndall, Mrs Gaskell and John Addington Symonds, the writer and critic, who married Marianne's sister Catherine in November 1864.

Mr North had many distinguished friends in the scientific, artistic, literary and political worlds, including personalities such as Sir Edward Sabine, the President of the Royal Society, George Bentham, the botanist, Francis Galton, the distinguished Victorian scientist, and Sir William Hooker (father of Sir Joseph, mentioned earlier), the Director of Kew Gardens. Marianne was able therefore to meet a wide circle of interesting and influential people, some of whom in later life, after the death of her father, were to stand her in good stead.

There is no doubt Mr North had a great interest in plants. He and Marianne often visited the Horticultural Society's Gardens at Chiswick as well as the Botanic Gardens at Kew, where their friend, Sir William Hooker, would show them wonderful tropical plants, many of which had been newly introduced to England. Once Marianne records that Sir William gave her a hanging bunch of flowers of *Amherstia nobilis*, a beautiful tree from Burma, which he described as 'the most strikingly superb object that can possibly be imagined'. Marianne thought it 'one of the grandest flowers in existence' and said it made her long more and more to see the tropics. At Hastings Mr North built three greenhouses, one for temperate plants, one for orchids and one for vines and cuttings. Marianne and her father would sometimes spend much of their time in the greenhouses where Marianne potted off the young seedlings and tended the ailing plants, while her father sat

Foliage and flowers of *Amherstia nobilis* painted in Singapore. Marianne called it 'one of the grandest flowers in existence' and it was seeing plants like this at Kew that made her long for the tropics.

peacefully smoking and reading in the 'temperate regions'. Although she had no formal education in botany, Marianne learnt much about plants from this close association and no doubt read a great deal about the subject at the same time. Marianne and her father became even closer after the marriage of her sister and went on many expeditions together. Once they got as far as Turkey,

Egypt and Syria, but they never managed to reach Marianne's longed-for tropics.

After the passion for music waned, Marianne became increasingly interested in painting. She had always taken the customary sketchbook on their travels and one year had spent the whole time painting all the fungi she could find. In 1850 she had her first lessons in flower painting from Magdalen von Fowinkel, a Dutch artist who had exhibited at the Royal Academy between 1831 and 1846 and who gave her ideas of colour and grouping. The following year Valentine Bartholomew (1799–1879), who was for many years flower painter in ordinary to Queen Victoria, gave her a few lessons in flower painting.

Hastings attracted a number of well-known artists, some of whom were permanent residents, while others spent part of the year there. Samuel Prout (1783–1852) lived in a lodging house for several years in a depressed state, mourning his absence from 'dearest and sweetest London'. Ill-health frequently confined him to bed, where he did many of his drawings. William Hunt (1790–1864) spent the winters at Hastings for thirty years, in a house which overlooked the beach. Marianne admired his pencil sketches of the boats and fishermen and longed to take lessons from him, but he would not teach her.

The remarkable Edward Lear (1812–1888) – ornithological draughtsman, landscape painter, traveller, musician and creator of nonsense rhymes – lodged for a time in their gardener's cottage. He used their fig tree and a raven strapped on to a branch of an apple tree as models for missing items in his pictures of the Quarries of Syracuse and Thermopylae. He would wander through

Frederick North reading in the garden at Hastings Lodge:
a painting by Marianne.

their french windows at dusk, sit down at the piano and sing Tennyson for hours, composing as he went and picking out the accompaniments by ear. Sometimes he would substitute nonsense words, much to Marianne's great amusement. He gave her great encouragement in her painting and remained a lifelong friend. 'The Owl and the Pussy-cat', probably Lear's best-known nonsense rhyme, was written for Janet Symonds, Marianne's niece. Lear wrote 'Their little girl is unwell – & all is sad'. Four days later he visited them with 'a picture poem for little Janet'.

The turning point in Marianne's artistic career came in 1867, when she was thirty-seven: she had her first lessons in oil painting from Robert Dowling (1827–1886), an Australian artist who had spent Christmas with them at Hastings. Up to that time she had always used watercolour, but once she had tried oils she developed a passion for it, and described it as 'a vice like dram-drinking, almost impossible to leave off once it gets possession of one'.

Her last visit with her father to Europe was in 1869. At Gastein, near Salzburg, Mr North became extremely ill and Marianne was advised to bring him home. The end came on 29 October, five days after Marianne's thirty-ninth birthday. His last words were 'Come give me a kiss, Pop, I am only going to sleep'. He never woke again and Marianne was left to face a world without her beloved father. 'For myself', she wrote to a friend, 'all is gone. I shall leave England as soon as possible.' She left Hastings Lodge 'for ever' and then made a trip to Europe with the family servant, Elizabeth. It was not a success. Marianne wanted to be alone and was increasingly irritated by Elizabeth while Elizabeth for her part just wanted to get home.

Back in England Marianne became utterly miserable – her 'one friend and idol of her life' had gone and she was left alone, not even wishing to talk of him or indeed of anything else. Her family were worried about her but could do nothing to help.

There was, apparently, no question of marriage – although her niece Margaret Symonds thought that many people must have wished to marry her and recorded that Marianne had asked one suitor to leave the room and then shut the door behind him. Of marriage Marianne once wrote 'it is a terrible experiment ... for a man especially, as a woman is something like your cat and gets to love the person who feeds her and the house she lives in, but men,

if they have brains, have a romantic idea of companionship in their wife and then discover they have no two ideas in common ... I pity the poor wife too when she finds herself snubbed, and a sort of upper servant to be scolded if the pickles are not right and then she will have to amuse herself by flirting with the most brainless of the Croquet-Badmintons'.

It was therefore a great relief to all concerned when, two years after her father's death, Marianne received an invitation from an American friend to stay with her in the United States. Marianne herself believed that this could be the first step to carrying out her plan for painting the wonders of the tropics and the trip was indeed the first of her epic journeys to 'paint the peculiar vegetation' of other lands. 1871 was thus a landmark in Marianne's life; a new life really did begin for her at forty.

'Pop' as a young woman; from her snapbook at Rougham.

Scadoxus multiflorus ssp
multiflorus, with coral snake
Micrurus species and spider,
in Brazil.

THE TRAVELS

In all her many journeys Marianne was fortunate to have letters of introduction to ambassadors, viceroys, rajahs, governors, ministers and other people of note. Wherever she went, English people and others befriended her and sent her on her way with further letters. No doubt the sight of an Englishwoman travelling alone caused plenty of comment and speculation. Although she spent some time staying in hotels, inns and boarding houses, she was as often being entertained in government residences or palaces or by friends or acquaintances in their own homes. Marianne was undoubtedly an intrepid and determined traveller and thought nothing of finding her way to totally out-of-the-way places, staying in the most primitive accommodation or experiencing the most diverse and often uncomfortable and dangerous forms of transport. It must be remembered too, that unlike many globe-trotters, Marianne not only had to get herself from place to place, but had to take all the equipment for her painting with her as well. Strangely she was often nervous on arriving at new places but, once the hurdle was overcome, her fear left her and her only concern was to find new things to paint.

Her travelling companions were often of very mixed account, although even the roughest seem to have recognized her as 'a lady' and treated her with respect. Marianne was passionately interested in people and revelled in meeting unusual or eccentric characters. She was willing to make friends with all races and classes of society; however, the imperious and autocratic Miss North could and did appear when the occasion necessitated. Stupidity, idleness and thoughtlessness she could not tolerate and, faced with these, she could plunge into 'one of those rages which are sometimes necessary'.

Her brother-in-law, John Addington Symonds, described her as 'blond, stout, tall, good humoured and a little satirical'. Marianne was bored and irritated by conventional 'society' people. She longed for stimulating conversation with intelligent and interesting scholars or Bohemians and valued good friends above all else; as she once remarked, they were the only real reason for wishing to live. She also loved all sorts of animals, as is very apparent from her letters and journals; she treated them with great respect and often imbued them with her own sentiments.

It was also fortunate that her father had left her well provided for so that she was able to travel to far-distant places without worrying about the expense. (Her bank, the famous Coutts, sent her money or made arrangements for her to obtain cash or credit in remote places.)

Mrs Skinner, the American friend who was to accompany Marianne on the trip across the Atlantic, seemed an ideal travelling companion for this first big venture. She was full of laughter and fun and, as Marianne remarked, did everyone good. She had curls of pure silver, topped with a 'purple cobweb', diamond earrings and an amazing quantity of luggage. She was able to divert and amuse Marianne and prevent her brooding excessively about her father.

On the whole Marianne did not care for intimate travelling companions and often contrived to drop them at the first opportunity. Although she needed good company, she could be just as happy on her own, fulfilling her life's ambition of painting her

View of Mrs Skinner's house in West Manchester, Massachusetts, with 'Indian corn'
in the foreground.

beloved plants in their natural habitats. She once said her greatest pleasure was to see new countries but that she equally enjoyed staying quietly at home, adding caustically that only ignorant fools thought because one liked sugar one couldn't like salt.

America and Canada

So it was with Mrs Skinner that Marianne had her first sight of a new continent. After crossing the Atlantic with a crowd of Second Class Irish and First Class Americans, whom Marianne found noisy and uninteresting, and struggling with Mrs Skinner's extraordinary quantity of luggage, the pair landed in Boston. Soon they ensconced themselves in a newly built house in West Manchester, where Marianne was in a state of continual excitement, surrounded by a wealth of new plants – scarlet lobelias, strange white orchids, sweet bay, ferns and all sorts of other delights, including little green humming-birds darting in and out of some of the flowers. The house was built on the foundations of an old fort and surrounded on three sides by the sea. Marianne and her companion bought material to make bathing dresses. Marianne's was dark blue-grey and Mrs Skinner's scarlet; Marianne remarked that they looked like two lobsters – one unboiled and the other boiled!

Eventually Marianne, Mrs Skinner and Mrs Skinner's luggage set off for Canada. They passed through glorious autumnal woods,

drank free iced water and marvelled at their travelling companions, which included a disgruntled cat who sat panting like a dog during the entire train journey. At Alton they took a steamer through the beautiful lake of Winnipesaukee and were dazzled by the red and crimson colours of the maples and sycamores on the countless islands. Then it was Quebec, which seemed to Marianne 'a mongrel sort of place', with English-looking streets, French quarters, Irish villages, Indian settlements and an odd climate and on to Montreal by steamer, up to La Chine by rail and back by steamer; then Ottawa, Kingston and Toronto and at last to the station hotel at Clifton and the Niagara Falls. It was here that Marianne finally rebelled.

She had been getting more and more irritated with Mrs Skinner, whose jolly moods were all too frequently interspersed with black ones. There were perpetual quarrels, scoldings and scenes and so when her companion declared her intention of going on to a grander hotel, Marianne told her she could do what she liked, but she, Marianne, was going to stay quietly in the station hotel for the next two weeks, resting and painting. Mrs Skinner's son was sent for; he removed his mother and Marianne was left in peace. (All references to Mrs Skinner's terrible tantrums were however taken out of Marianne's memoirs when they were published after her death.)

Niagara far exceeded her grandest ideas and she was in an agony of indecision as to what to paint first – she was almost too excited to start painting at all. However she eventually settled herself on some boulders between the two roaring falls, idly wondering if anyone would notice if she fell and was borne away by the roaring torrent. As usual she made friends with those around her; the Head Guide of the Falls and his wife offered her cups of coffee if she got cold, the woman at the tollgate refused to take any money, and some of the other tourists wanted to know what price she would get for her paintings.

New York was very expensive. Marianne's ride of a quarter of a mile from station to hotel cost eight shillings, dresses were three to four hundred dollars and gloves ten shillings a pair. No wonder, said Marianne, the Americans went to Europe for their shopping. Another friend, Mrs Botta, took her to exhibitions and introduced her to several artists including Frederick Edwin Church (1826–1900) who showed her many of his paintings including his studies of tropical scenes.

In Washington Marianne stayed with the Gurneys and it was here, much to both the Gurneys' and Marianne's astonishment, that she received an invitation to dine at the White House. To her alarm, she was armed in to dinner by President Grant, who sat next to her, drank tea with his dinner, and uttered few words or, as Marianne put it, had 'a great talent for silence'. Later they found it was all a question of mistaken identity – they had imagined her to be the daughter of Lord North, one-time Prime Minister of England, which would have made her absurdly antique. After attending the opening of the Congress, Marianne returned to New York, which was beginning to get very cold and where snow had already fallen. It was therefore with relief and joy that on 15 December she boarded a steamer bound for Jamaica.

Within a week she was experiencing that unique tropical warmth, blankets were dispensed with and a single sheet proved almost unendurable. She was intensely excited by her first sight of the luscious tropical vegetation, as they entered the Bay of Kingston. This was a land she had been dreaming of all those years ago when she had wandered through the exotic Palm House at Kew with her father and Sir William Hooker.

Jamaica

It was Christmas Eve when Marianne arrived in Jamaica. She described herself as 'entirely alone and friendless', but it was not for long. Almost immediately a young Cuban engineer swept up Marianne and her luggage and took her to an hotel nearby. Here the Jamaican landlady gave up her own room as there were no others free. Christmas found Marianne in the middle of a tropical market, surrounded by Jamaican ladies sporting their gayest dresses decorated with pink, orange and red satin bows, with feathers and artificial flowers in their hair and baskets of cakes and fruit balanced on their heads. Marianne tasted her first mango, a fruit she thought unequalled. By the time she returned to the hotel, word had got round of her arrival, and she found a Dr Campbell waiting to take her off to stay with him and his wife. The Campbells were very hospitable, and untiring in their kindness, but Marianne soon made her escape for, as she once wrote, 'I am a very wild bird and like liberty'.

She rented a twenty-roomed house in the old deserted Botanic Garden for four pounds a month and hired enough furniture for two rooms. She bought an enormous bunch of ninety bananas for eighteen pence which she hung up like a chandelier and hired two old Jamaican servants to look after her. Every week Marianne bought two pounds of beef from the soldiers' guardhouse and each day she stewed some up with fresh vegetables. She ate her way steadily through the bananas, but eventually the string broke and the whole lot crashed to the ground and so the rest were given to the pigs.

From her verandah she had a magnificent view of the steep wooded valley and the meadows, while all around the house there was a tangle of all sorts of exotic plants. There were bananas, palms, breadfruit and mahogany trees, gorgeous tree ferns, orchids, bromeliads, allamandas, bignonias, passion flowers and ipomoeas climbing over everything. She wrote, 'I was in a state of ecstasy, and hardly knew what to paint first'. However she settled herself into a routine of going out to paint at daylight and returning home at midday. She spent the afternoon painting indoors, when there was heavy rain outside, and, when it had cleared, she went out to explore, returning home in the dark. Sometimes, when her servants were out, she was left completely alone, 'with silvery banana leaves

The valley behind Marianne's house at Gordontown, Jamaica, with *Brugmansia arborea* in the foreground.

RIGHT: Foliage, flowers and fruit of coffee, Jamaica. Marianne described coffee as 'an ill-regulated shrub', with its berries ripening at different times.

OPPOSITE: Group of wild and cultivated flowers, Jamaica. In the centre *Portlandia grandiflora* with white flowers, and morning glory, *Ipomoea tricolor*; above the latter *Bougainvillea spectabilis*, the blue *Duranta erecta*, a *Heliotropium (? indicum)* and *Hippeastrum reginae*. On the right from the top: the orchid, *Encyclia cochleata*, *Syzygium jambos*, *Hibiscus rosa-sinensis* and a member of the Acanthaceae. The branch lying in front belongs to the celebrated lace-bark tree, *Lagetta lintearia*.

View in the Fernwalk, Jamaica, at an elevation of 5,000 feet.

flapping against the shutters, the fireflies darting, and the glow-worms crawling all round'. The one thing she did dislike were the revivalists who used to 'howl and talk unknown tongues and foam at the mouth' for hours at a time, sometimes even continuing throughout the night. The crickets and frogs also had a nightly revival meeting, and rivalled 'the bipeds in the noise that they made', but what they said, Marianne remarked, probably had more sense and meaning.

In this way she enjoyed a month of complete quiet and incessant painting, but then people began to find her out and invitations to stay poured in. The Governor, Sir Peter John Grant, invited her to stay at Craigton, a pleasant little house which had a beautiful view, like an opal, over Kingston and Port Royal. The garden was ablaze with colour – red dracaenas, poinsettias and the famous *Amherstia nobilis*.

She was interested in all the many economic plants she saw and not only painted their portraits with her brush but wrote detailed descriptions of them with her pen. It has sometimes been said that her pen was almost as mighty as her brush. There was coffee, with all its berries ripening at different times, cocoa, with tiny flowers and huge pods hanging directly from the trunk, and nutmeg with the fruits just opening and showing the crimson network of mace around the seed. Rum she saw being made and sometimes being drunk too freely and remarked that it was the curse of the country. Some of the bamboos were crushed and made into a coarse kind of paper. Marianne lamented the destruction of these graceful plants but felt no one cared.

The birds and other creatures were a never-ending source of interest – banana birds and Jamaica robins, lizards who sat sunning themselves on the walls, and land crabs, one of which she encountered in her bedroom, and afterwards ate for her supper 'all minced up in his own shell'. The rats however she did not care for, as one night they ate holes in her precious boots, so for the rest of the stay she always placed the boots on top of the water jug out of

View of the Bay of Rio and the Sugarloaf Mountain, Brazil.

reach of rodent teeth. She seemed greatly to enjoy all her new food experiences. At the Governor's she tried fresh ginger pudding, tomato toast, fried ackee (*Blighia sapida*), mango stew, coconut cream and roast turtle and 'many other things not heard of in Europe'. She drank 'matrimony', a delicious mixture of star-apple, sugar and Seville orange juice, which tasted like strawberry cream.

After five months on this exotic island, Marianne returned home and for the next two months enjoyed the society of her many friends in London recounting tales of her new-found tropical world. On 9 August 1872 however the adventurous Miss North was off on her travels again, this time bound for Brazil.

Brazil

By early September Marianne was ensconced in a large airy room in the Hôtel des Etrangers at Botafogo on the outskirts of Rio, with a perfect view of the Sugar Loaf and the Corcovado Mountains. Sir Joseph Hooker had told her 'the hotel was a hole unfit for xtiens [Christians] and the landlord a rogue', but Marianne did not believe him and never repented going there. In any case, she felt she could put up with any hovel to stay and paint in such a glorious country.

Rio was very colourful and the houses somewhat reminiscent of Spain and Sicily. The inhabitants had the same love of hanging out gaudy draperies and flowers from their windows, only here with the addition of parrots and monkeys screaming and scrambling after the passers-by. Every morning at six am Marianne took the mule-car to the famous Botanic Garden nearby, where she made a study of a remarkable avenue of royal palms, which was said to be half a mile in length. The Austrian Director allowed Marianne to keep her easel and other equipment in his house and shouted angrily at anyone who got between Marianne and the subject she was painting.

As usual Marianne fell on her feet, for on an expedition to the

Study of the traveller's tree, *Ravenala madagascariensis*, in the Botanic Garden at
Rio, Brazil.

Corcovado Mountains she had the good fortune to meet a Mr Gordon, the manager of a mine, and his daughter, Mary. This resulted in an invitation to stay with them at their home at Morro Velho in Minas Gerais. The weather was particularly wet at the time and the mud indescribably awful and all her friends in Rio were against her making the trip. One assured her there was nothing to paint, another said she would find the scenery very monotonous, while yet another declared that the route was impassable and that travellers were being turned back. Marianne however was not to be deterred.

Part of the journey was undertaken in a carriage drawn by four mules which went so fast that Marianne was not able to appreciate the superb scenery and longed to dismount. There were magnificent tall trees – scarlet erythrinas and orange-flowered cassias draped with bougainvilleas – ferns, begonias, arums, agaves and many other wonders. At Juiz de Fora thirty-seven mules were loaded up with luggage and riders for the great journey to the Gordons' home. The weather was terrible and the mules stumbled into the liquid mud holes or became so stuck that they had to be lifted out bodily by head and tail. Once the mule in front of Marianne flopped into the mud up to its neck and a man was ordered to carry Marianne on his back. However with her extra

Side avenue of royal palms, *Roystonea regia*,
at Botafogo, Brazil.

Flowers of *Bombax marginatum*, a Brazilian forest tree,
revealing its long, showy stamens.

Brazil: foliage and flowers of bougainvillea, with a bird, the Brazilian ruby, *Clytolaema rubinea*.

Landscape at Morro Velho, Brazil. In the foreground is a colony of butterflies, *Heliconius erato phyllis*, going to roost on a single segment of a palm leaf, from which they will never move until the sun's rays reach them in the morning. The insect has a powerful musk-like scent which often attracted Marianne to it.

Yellow bignonia, *Bignonia aequinoctialis*, and swallow-tail butterflies, *Papilio thoas*, with a view of Congonhas, Brazil.

The aqueduct of Morro Velho, Brazil, with the Coral Mountains in the background; in the foreground part of an inflorescence of a banana, with a species of *Ipomoea* and amethyst woodstar (*Calliphlox amethystina*) birds.

Wildflowers at Morro Velho, Brazil. *Bignonia venusta* and *Quamoclit nationis* climbing over *Luhea rufescens*, a forest tree.

weight (which she remarked was no light one) he sank further into the mire and so Marianne scrambled back on to her mule, Mueda, 'who stood steady as a rock, and seemed to grin to herself at the idea of anyone but herself having the strength to carry me'. In some small towns conditions were so terrible that many of the inhabitants had not been out for a month or more. Often the travellers were soaked to the skin and found it difficult to dry out. Marianne's attire consisted of a short linsey petticoat, a long waterproof cloak and an old black straw hat, while on her pommel, she carried a rolled-up silk waterproof 'for extra wet hours'.

Eventually they arrived at Casa Grande, the Gordons' home. She had agreed to spend two weeks with the Gordons but in retrospect they laughed for she stayed eight months. It was an artist's paradise with a garden filled with beautiful plants and in the woods nearby there were banks of sensitive plants (*Mimosa pudica*), wild ginger, whose flowers scented the whole air, and enormous castor oil plants. The Gordons kept a number of pets including two macaws, one blue with a yellow breast, the other red and green, who was a great friend of the cat. Marianne recorded that these two strange friends used to huddle close together, scratching each other's heads. Occasionally after over-zealous scratching, there were rows and noisy arguments in 'macawese and cat languages'. Marianne's greatest friend was the mongrel dog, Lopez, who used to accompany her into the forest, clearing the way and 'giving all enemies [such as snakes] notice to quit'. She delighted in all the wildlife she encountered, particularly the gorgeous blue and opal morpho butterflies which flapped their great wide wings with a kind of see-saw motion, the spiders 'as big as sparrows' and the awkward sloths which crept slowly along the branches of trees.

The Highlands of Brazil brought Marianne fresh wonders. She and the Gordons spent some months there, visiting friends or staying at inns or other lodgings. Once Marianne spent a fortnight virtually alone in a deserted house, going out early each morning on her mule to find some choice spot in the forest to paint, and returning 'in time for a good wash before dinner'. The accommodation she encountered was very varied. Sometimes she was lodged in the best rooms with every luxury, tubs of water, embroidered towels, sumptous meals and 'the best of coffee'. At

Flowers and fruit of the maricojas passion flower, *Passiflora alata*, Brazil.

LEFT: A white-flowered bladderwort, *Utricularia alpina*, an epiphytic carnivorous plant, with the Brazilian *Sinningia concinna*.

View of the Old Gold Works from the verandah of Mr Gordon's house at Morro Velho, Brazil,
with *Magnolia grandiflora* and various pet animals in the foreground.

other times conditions were excessively primitive. At Ribera, she had, she said, 'a very tolerable mud-floored room to myself, and a quantity of pigeons pattering over the mat (which did duty for a ceiling over my head), cooing to each other and kicking down dust and fleas ...' It was all a very far cry from her comfortable Victorian world, but she seemed to enjoy it to the full, often relishing describing the awfulness of her experiences in letters home.

Eventually all good things come to an end and soon Marianne was steaming towards England in company with nine little singing birds which she kept on the spare berth in her cabin. Marianne spent the next few months back in England learning to etch on copper and enjoying the company of her increasing number of friends. It was an unusually cold winter and Marianne found the weather quite unbearable.

Tenerife

On 1 January 1875 Marianne set off with her friend, Mary Ewart, for Tenerife and the sun and warmth. After a fortnight on the island Miss Ewart left and Marianne then settled down to paint in earnest.

The people were very friendly and once they discovered Marianne was a painter, brought her quantities of beautiful specimens. She met Spanish noblemen and women with 'the very bluest of blood' and the loveliest of gardens and enjoyed the picturesque costume of many of the inhabitants – the men with high top boots, blankets round their necks and huge Rubens-style hats and the women with their red and black petticoats and bright-coloured shawls. She visited Oratava, Puerto and Santa Cruz; in Icod she was taken to see the fine views by a Spanish nobleman who, much to Marianne's embarrassment, insisted on walking arm

OPPOSITE: Group of 'wild meadow flowers' of Brazil with golden banana and greater ani or euemba (*Crotophaga major*) egg. The flowers include a white *Clusia*, a species of *Tibouchina* and *Thunbergia alata* (yellow with dark centre).

RIGHT: View of the Peak of Tenerife with prickly pear cacti (*Opuntia*) and other succulent plants in the foreground; on the right the century plant, *Agave americana*, in flower.

Opuntia dillenii, a species of prickly pear, whose spikes are used to fasten the bags of cochineal insects to another species on which the insects are found. The reddish flowers are those of *Canarina canariensis* and the violet-blue ones are a species of *Iochroma*. The birds are red-faced lovebirds, *Agapornis pullaria*.

The Cherokee rose, *Rosa laevigata*, and a pink semi-double damask rose with the Peak of Tenerife in the distance. The Cherokee rose is native to South China and Taiwan, but has long been cultivated elsewhere.

in arm with her over ploughed fields and slippery pavements which were at an angle of forty-five degrees!

She was particularly impressed with the dragon trees, *Dracaena draco*, and made several studies of them, although she lamented that they were bled so often for the dye, known as dragon's blood. In one area she was at first perplexed by what appeared to be a 'paper bun bag harvest'. On closer inspection she found it was a cochineal plantation with white rags covering hatching insects on trays pinned on to the prickly pear cactus.

America

By May she was back in London and by August she was off to Japan via America with new-found friends who had in fact suggested the trip. Marianne had some pithy comments to make about her fellow passengers; there was 'a mighty deal of heavy leaven among them – men who looked like rich butchers and wool collectors; the women with odd rings on their forefingers'. They journeyed to Quebec, and on to Chicago and Salt Lake by train; then it was fourteen hours in a horrible springless machine which jolted along the terrible and dusty roads. At least the fearful crowding prevented bones being broken, but it did not stop the tiresome maid Marie being 'sea sick'..

Soon Marianne forgot all this when she had her first sight of 'THE TREES', the giant redwoods or wellingtonias (*Sequoiadendron giganteum*) and then many hours were spent painting in both Mariposa and Calaveras Groves, sometimes with only a stag for company. She also visited the forests of coastal redwoods (*Sequoia sempervirens*) and lamented their terrible destruction for firewood. San Francisco she described as 'a strange mixture of new Paris streets and Irish hovels, with its still stranger Chinese town in one corner'. She spent a week in a comfortable hotel in the Nevada Mountains where she was very happy painting by herself and enjoying the lovely air. Once she found her refreshment had been put in an unwashed bottle of Harvey's Sauce and, although the taste was unpleasant, laughed until the tears ran down her face.

As usual she made friends with many of her drivers; one was a villainous-looking bandit who turned out to have a great admiration for Marianne's fearless nature and declared she was 'one

OPPOSITE: View of the Cochineal Gardens at Santa Cruz – 'The paper bun-bag harvest' – showing trays of cochineal insects pinned to *Opuntia cochenillifera*, a species of prickly pear.

LEFT: 'A fallen giant': the giant redwood or wellingtonia, *Sequoiadendron giganteum*, in Calaveras Grove, California.

LEFT: Wildflowers of California: in front the curious thistle-leaved sage, *Salvia carduacea*, with a species of *Calochortus* on the right; a scarlet catchfly, *Silene californica*, and species of *Phlox* above; and American cowslip, *Dodecatheon meadia*, on the left.

OPPOSITE: View of Lake Donner, Sierra Nevada, with the Great Pacific Railway on the right.

Distant view of Mount Fujiyama, Japan, framed by the beautiful climbing
shrub, *Wisteria sinensis*, a native of China and first introduced
to Britain in 1816.

A view of Kyoto in the morning mist from outside Marianne's paper window.

of the right sort' and 'neither cared for bears nor yet Ingins'. Another driver, a peculiar morose and seemingly silent character known as the 'Colonel', suddenly astonished Marianne by appearing at supper in a white waistcoat and dress coat and amused her with a flow of interesting talk.

Marianne delayed her departure for Japan when she found a woman and three children were to share her cabin and promptly went on shore again; her friends were left to go on ahead. However she eventually set off in the steamer *Oceania*, but found the journey too cold for her liking and the presence of a number of dead Chinamen (being returned to their homeland) made the atmosphere none too pleasant. For once, the people on board were congenial and entertaining and, in particular, Marianne was amused by a lively little lady 'in the tightest of dresses and highest of heeled boots' who was the life and soul of the party. Marianne had her first sight of Japan at daybreak on 7 November with a glorious view of Mount Fujiyama, which she later painted, framed with hanging wisteria.

Japan

Everything in Japan was strange and unlike anything Marianne had ever seen before. The houses were excessively neat and exquisitely finished and all on a miniature scale. They often had bamboo frames, paper windows and little stacks of rice straw piled round as extra padding against the cold; some even had beds of lilies on their roofs. The temples were like palaces of wood, richly gilded and

Japanese flowers. A yellow-flowered *Forsythia suspensa*, with members of the genera *Rhododendron* and *Camellia* with the moutan, *Paeonia suffruticosa*. The variegated foliage belongs to *Cleyera fortunei*.

Gate of the Mariamma temple, Japan. Marianne was particularly impressed by the many wonderful temples she saw, some filled with 'exquisite bronzes, china, and fresh flowers'.

painted inside, often surrounded by groups of Japanese cedars, pines and bamboos. The tea houses and their gardens were a delight; yellow sugarless tea or cherry blossom tea was served in tiny handleless cups, with delicate little cakes made of rice and bean flour. The countryside was looking spectacular that November; the maples were turning every tint of red, crimson, scarlet or deepest purple, and the leaves of the old ginkgo were beginning to change to a lovely yellow. Marianne used vast quantities of madder and carmine trying to 'imitate that which could not be imitated'.

Marianne had hoped to stay until the summer in Japan, for as she wrote to her friend, Maggie Shaen, 'these wonderful islands and their people are too full of attractions for me to leave in a hurry' but it was too cold and sometimes she could hardly stand or even hold her paint brush, from stiffness and oncoming rheumatism. She also

had an attack of her 'wretched old enemy' – gallstones – and once the pain was so great that she had to send for an American doctor, who 'squirted morphine into my arm and put me to sleep for 24 hours'. As usual she inspired devotion in those around her. Her Japanese 'boy', aged sixty, had a sword inside his walking stick with which he said 'he will kill anyone [who] no likee his Missus'. In Kyoto she stayed in an hotel which had once been a temple. Her room was made of paper with sliding panels all around, but the only trouble was that she could not see through the paper windows – if she opened them it let the cold air and damp rain in. Like many travellers, Marianne was tempted into buying all sorts of unnecessary objects and confessed she could 'commit bankruptcy on the teapots alone'.

It was in Japan that Marianne experienced one of her more

The durian fruit, *Durio zibethinus*, painted in Sarawak (see page 46). It 'smells like hell but tastes of heaven' and is also known as the civet cat fruit.

extraordinary modes of transport; this was the jinricksha, a kind of grown-up perambulator, which was dragged along by small Japanese men who went as 'quick as ponies'. These strange contraptions were much begilded and decorated and the men who pulled them were richly tattooed all over. Once, when returning from an expedition, Marianne's three 'bipeds' got into such a state of excitement that they started yelling like wild things and went at full gallop until they all fell down like 'like a pack of cards'. Marianne felt her head go crack against a wall and wondered if her end had come. When she picked herself up she found she was surrounded by a crowd of people all 'holding their sides and roaring with laughter'.

By 19 December Marianne could stand the cold no longer and decided to return to Yokohama. Here she stayed with friends and was in the care of a doctor for ten days, suffering from rheumatic fever. She was unable to feed herself and so hired a tiny, but tyrannical, nurse who kept her 'half starved on one roasted lark'. Marianne felt the only way she would recover was to seek the warmth of the tropics and so she travelled on to Singapore.

Singapore

Here she began to revive and although she could barely hobble, started to make a study of a great breadfruit tree which blocked her hotel window. Soon a banker's wife and her father persuaded the invalid to stay with them in their comfortable house outside the town. Under the tuition of some English children she learned to love that most notorious of all the fruits of the East, the durian, which has been described as 'smelling like hell and tasting of

Flowers and fruit of the cocoa tree, *Theobroma cacao*,
painted in Singapore.

Flowers and fruit of the star-fruit, *Averrhoa carambola*,
with butterflies (*Amblypodia*).

OPPOSITE: Foliage and flowers of the flame of the forest or flamboyant tree,
Delonix regia, Singapore. Marianne nearly fell into the trap of painting the
flowers upside-down, as a fellow artist had done.

LEFT: Foliage and flowers of *Medinilla magnifica*, native to the Philippines but cultivated in Singapore.

OPPOSITE: View of Kuching and the river, Sarawak, with the traveller's tree, *Ravenala madagascariensis*, on the left, coconut palms behind and *Nypa fruticans* in front.

heaven'. Of its aphrodisiac properties, it is said when the durians fall down the sarongs go up!

Marianne visited the Botanic Gardens, where superb untouched forest merged into the gardens. There were real pitcher plants (*Nepenthes*), the first she had seen growing wild, and she screamed with delight (as she did on frequent occasions). Later she stayed at Government House with Sir William and Lady Jervois and was soon furnished with letters of introduction for the next stage of her journey.

Sarawak (Borneo)

Marianne's trip to Sarawak in 1876 is of particular interest as there is not only her description of the visit, but that of the Ranee of Sarawak with whom she stayed in Kuching. The Ranee was an English girl who at the age of twenty had married the forty-year-old Charles Brooke (1849–1917), a nephew of the first 'White Rajah' and a rajah himself. Rajah Charles Brooke was a strong-minded Englishman, who dedicated his life to his adopted country and believed his mission was to preserve Sarawak from the exploitation and influence of the Europeans. He lived in some style with one hundred soldiers, a band which played every night, and about twenty men known as 'the officers', who came to play croquet every Tuesday. He had married Margaret de Windt primarily to provide himself and Sarawak with an heir. The Ranee produced a succession of offspring but by the time of Marianne's visit only 'one small tyrant of eighteen months' remained; the other three had died from cholera on the journey back to England. The Rajah's 'palace', the Istana, was a brick-built structure which stood on a little hill overlooking the river and was surrounded on three sides by tropical forest. The house was cool and comfortable and had an excellent library with books collected by the first Rajah,

The Istana, the Rajah of Sarawak's 'palace', from the slanting bridge, with gardenias, *Crinum northianum* (named after Marianne), *Nypa fruticans*, the betel-nut palm, *Areca catechu*, and bamboos in the foreground.

LEFT: The future Rajah of Sarawak, Charles Vyner Brooke, sitting under a stag's horn fern, probably *Platycerium holttumii*, with his attendants.

OPPOSITE: Pineapple, *Ananas comosus*, in flower and fruit, Sarawak. Marianne delighted in eating all the tropical fruit. In the Seychelles she recorded that sixteen large 'pines' could be bought for sixpence.

The oleander, *Nerium odorum*, native to tropical Asia, but cultivated in many parts of the world for its beautiful flowers. All parts of the plant are poisonous.

newspapers and every European luxury. The bedrooms even had bathrooms attached, *en suite*, as the Ranee rather grandly described them. The 'bath' consisted of filling a basket, made of *Nypa* palm leaves, with river water scooped from a large cistern, and pouring this over oneself.

The Ranee was delighted to have a guest to stay, as life was undoubtedly very monotonous for her. The days passed with the same routine – lawn tennis, croquet, constitutional walks and occasional dinner parties when the guests and music were always the same. The Ranee described Marianne as tall, lean and fair, with hair hardly tinged grey, a large nose, thin lips, blue spectacles and – was it said with some satisfaction? – not good looking. She also made several observations about Marianne's dress – she apparently sported a topi, very short petticoats, a light woollen jacket and high, heel-less wellington boots. Her 'undraped knees' were mentioned several times so the Ranee obviously thought them somewhat risqué.

Although the Ranee was pleased to see Marianne, she found her very exhausting. Even on Marianne's first day she described her as hurtlingly energetic, bustling about, arranging all her equipment and tying up the lace curtains so she could see the view outside. Marianne had brought three easels, all different in size, two or three large palettes, two enormous cases of completed pictures, and boxes and boxes full of paint brushes, charcoals and tubes of oils. The Ranee was used to having a siesta in the middle of the day, which Marianne found inexplicable when there were all these exotic sights around her. Marianne was astonished too that the Ranee had never heard of pitcher plants, but this was soon put right with a trip to a nearby jungle. Her hostess seemed irritated by Marianne's knowledge of plants and tried to impress her by making up bogus Latin names. Not for one moment was Marianne deceived and the Ranee was given a kindly scolding and told the name was nonsense!

The Ranee fancied herself as a pianist and often accompanied the Rajah's uncertain and out-of-tune tenor at musical evenings – it was *always* 'La Donna e Mobile' – but was piqued that nobody ever asked her for a solo. However the tables were turned when Marianne, spying a piano, asked her to play. The Ranee prepared to perform a movement of Beethoven's *Pathétique*, only to be told Marianne couldn't 'bear Beethoven in bits'. Somewhat annoyed,

Flowers of *Tacca cristata* (note the long, thread-like bracts arising from below the flowers) with the rambutan, *Nephelium lappaceum*, a delicious fruit related to the lychee, *Litchi chinensis*.

A group of cultivated flowers. In the foreground *Dendrobium primulinum* and *Combretum grandiflorum*, with a passion flower, *Passiflora laurifolia*, and a white-flowered *Bauhinia variegata*, a *Crinum* species, and *Ixora coccinea* in the jar. The drooping yellow flowers are those of *Gmelina hystrix* and the purple flowers are *Asystasia coromandeliana*.

OPPOSITE: Flowers and fruit of pomelo or shaddock, *Citrus grandis*, with branch of henna, *Lawsonia inermis*, the well-known dye plant, and flying lizard, *Draco volans*.

Forest scene at Matang, Sarawak, with black apes swinging from the lianes. Marianne got a good view of them through her opera glass.

the Ranee obliged and managed to play the whole work. Marianne then sang several songs to her wilting hostess, who by this time was longing for her bed!

There was a certain amount of friction between the Rajah and Marianne as both fancied themselves as botanists and gardeners. There were arguments over identifications and methods of cultivation and the Ranee quaintly remarked that tempers always seemed to be raised when there was curry for dinner!

Marianne had at last got rid of her Japanese rheumatism and could paint and move about with ease. Sometimes she worked in her room or in the garden; at other times there were trips into the jungle, often by canoe, when she would stay away for several days. The forests were a perfect world of wonders with lycopodiums, orchids, pitcher plants of every size, and black apes who swung on the lianes. In letters home, she particularly delighted in describing the pitcher plants: 'I have two now a foot and a half long – one of them bright rose in colour'. One of these proved to be a new species and was named *Nepenthes northiana* in her honour.

Java

Java was Marianne's 'next treat' that year and it certainly came up to her expectations. In fact she considered it surpassed Brazil, Jamaica and Sarawak all put together. Not only were there luxuriant forests, lakes filled with the sacred lotus and vast plains of rice, indigo, corn, manioc, tea and tobacco, but there were fantastic buildings and the most impressive volcanoes. Marianne particularly approved of the houses made of woven rattan or bamboo often set on stilts. She found the Javanese a handsome race, and much admired their brightly coloured clothes and was amused by the universal habit of carrying an umbrella at all times.

In Bogor she stayed in a hotel only fifteen minutes' walk from the Botanic Garden and soon made friends with the Director who provided her with all the flowers she wanted. From her hotel window she enjoyed watching the local children dressed in nothing but a banana leaf, on their heads, and the old men flying kites with 'their gray [sic] beards thrown up in the air, and their respectable turbans falling off their heads'.

Marianne left Bogor for Jakarta with 'a big letter in her pocket' from the Governor General to all officials, native and Dutch,

The view from Marianne's window at Bogor, Java, with coconut palms, bananas,
breadfruit trees and coffee bushes. *Clerodendron paniculatum* is in flower on the left.

OPPOSITE ABOVE: *Ficus benjamina* in the Great Square at Malang, Java, with bullock carts beneath.

OPPOSITE BELOW: Banyan trees, *Ficus benghalensis*, at Bogor, Java, showing the aerial roots descending from the branches and eventually forming 'a little forest in itself'.

RIGHT: Foliage and flowers of the clove, *Syzygium aromaticum*, with mango fruit and statue of the Hindu god of wisdom.

asking them to feed and lodge her and pass her on to wherever she wanted to go. And go she did to endless places in Java. She inspected Hindu ruins, sometimes with an official holding a gilt umbrella of state over her head, much to her embarrassment. From the monastery at Borobudur, she had a most magnificent view of the Soembing volcano and nearby she was amazed to see about four hundred sitting statues of the Buddha. Everywhere the people seemed interested in Marianne's painting. Most watched her quietly, but the Chinese children crowded round her in a most unpleasant throng. One boy came so close and stared so hard that Marianne 'calmly raised [her] paint brush a little and put a dab of blue at the end of his nose, and the applause in the street below was uproarious!'

Marianne's abiding memory of Java must surely have been of the lively horses and ponies, on which she sometimes rode for hours at a time. It was fortunate that she was an accomplished horsewoman, as some of the ponies had 'a habit of resisting their riders' getting on their backs and 'showing fight at first', but were excellent and untirable once started.

On one occasion Marianne was warned that the only horse to be had was 'peculiar', a mild term, she considered for 'he required three men to hold his head when I mounted the next morning, and two to lead him the first mile, after which he tossed me off and tried to macadamise me ... I felt death was coming, and felt quite comfortable ... I had no fear, only wished it over. Then the stirrup-leather broke, and the brute got out of my way, and I got up none the worse'. The practical Miss North then comforted the man who had led the horse, and set about making a new stirrup with a twisted bamboo rope and remounted her steed. Marianne was often amused by these incidents and once recorded that they had all laughed including the pony. Sometimes she travelled with great Javanese officials in their grand carriages pulled by horses which went like the wind, and perpetually seemed to be 'trying to catch some phantom train'. It was all a breathless experience but one which Marianne enjoyed to the full.

Sri Lanka

Marianne left Java in the same steamer which had brought her there, bound for Sri Lanka via Singapore. As usual she found many of her fellow passengers very trying – in particular there was one dreadful woman with high-heeled boots who had two parrots and a baby. The baby was placed between the parrots who deliberately bit

View in the Royal Botanic Gardens, Peradeniya, Sri Lanka, with bamboos and jak fruit, *Artocarpus heterophylla*, in the foreground.

Foliage and fruit of the tamarind, *Tamarindus indica* (the pulp is an essential
ingredient of Worcestershire sauce), and flower and fruit of the papaw,
Carica papaya.

the child until it screamed with pain. Whereupon the woman cuffed all three, which resulted in even more uproar. The company on the boat from Singapore to Sri Lanka was also uncongenial – Dutch, Chinese and a group of mixed Britishers, who either sulked or were totally silent.

It was therefore with relief that Marianne arrived at Galle, where she stayed for ten days marvelling at all she saw around her and delighting in the sight of a bright green chameleon with a long tail and scarlet comb. She did not however delight in her fellow countrymen, whom she described as an unchoice collection much given to 'brandy and soda'. Marianne identified herself with a bored monkey who had to go through all his tricks for the benefit of the newly arrived passengers whom he appeared to despise totally. However he obviously recognized Marianne's worth and shook her by the hand on a day when he was not having to entertain.

Colombo she found cooler but unattractive and stayed there for only a few days. She went on to Kandy, the old capital, and admired the beautiful scenery as the train climbed slowly up to the top of the pass, noting in particular the *Caryota* palms with their fishtail-shaped leaves. It was dark and raining when Marianne arrived at her hotel and no one helped her with her luggage. She admitted to getting in a rage and scolding the idle natives but was eventually given a room, tea and a plate of half-cold, hard salt-beef and carrots. Early next morning she set out for the famous Botanic Gardens at Peradeniya, an idyllic spot with the river winding round the garden. Her letters of introduction resulted in her leaving the hotel and staying nearby with Judge Laurie, a most happy arrangement as the Judge was often away. Here she painted to her heart's delight, away from Kandy, which she described as a 'cockney' sort of place full of croquet, lawn tennis and scandals. It was, she conceded, a pretty town with the artificial lake in the centre and the great Temple of the Tooth, where Marianne tried to paint in semi-darkness one day.

It was while in Sri Lanka in January 1877 that Marianne met Julia Margaret Cameron, the famous photographer, who invited her to stay at Kalutara. Although Mrs Cameron was no great beauty and something of an eccentric, Marianne found her oddities most refreshing after 'the don't care attitude' of so many she had met. The two women had much in common – both independent

Clump of bamboos, *Dendrocalamus giganteus*, in the Royal Botanic Gardens, Peradeniya, Sri Lanka, planted in 1852.

OPPOSITE: *Ipomoea pes-caprae*, a common plant on sandy shores in the tropics; it will sometimes grow 100 feet in length.

Bombay pedlars on the verandah of Julia Margaret Cameron's house at
Kalutara, Sri Lanka.

minded, both taking up their life's work late in life and both despising the conventions of society. Mrs Cameron did not begin her career in photography until she was forty-eight years old when she was given a camera by her daughter. The thought of photographing Marianne put Mrs Cameron in a fever of excitement and the story of the sitting has been told many times. Marianne was dressed in flowing draperies of cashmere wool, told to let her hair down, and, with spiky coconuts running into her head, the noonday sun dodging her eyes and the temperature at ninety-six degrees, was told 'to look perfectly natural'. Mrs Cameron, Marianne noted, wasted twelve plates and 'an enormous amount of trouble' but only succeeded in getting a 'perfectly uninteresting and commonplace person'.

Marianne eventually arrived back in England in late February 1877. A few months later she was delighted to receive a visit from the Emperor and Empress of Brazil who climbed all her stairs to view her paintings. Another exciting event was an invitation to lend her paintings for an exhibition at the Kensington Museum. She had planned to go to India and so spent her last few weeks in England making a catalogue of her sketches and adding notes about their natural history, of which she found people woefully ignorant.

A photograph of Marianne 'dressed in flowing draperies' taken by the famous photographer, Julia Margaret Cameron, in Sri Lanka in January 1877.

Jak fruit, *Artocarpus heterophylla*, eaten as fruit or vegetable, and sometimes weighing up to 100 pounds.

Foliage, flowers and fruit of *Bauhinia variegata*, a common Indian forest tree.

Foliage and flowers of two Indian rhododendrons, *Rhododendron griffithianum*, with white flowers and *R arboreum*, the commonest mountain species.

Street in Ajmere and the Gate of the Daghar Mosque, India.

India

In September 1877 Marianne set off for India (via Sri Lanka) where she stayed over a year, gradually wending her way from south to north and enjoying the countless new plants, the exotic architecture and the diverse people. Edward Lear had shown Marianne many of his Indian sketches and had no doubt fired her imagination with his enthusiastic descriptions of the country. He told her of the beautiful places 'whose vegetation was enough to make tadpoles screech with delight'. In 1877 there had been a total failure of crops in southern and western India and on arrival Marianne found starvation, floods and fever all around and many of the people were 'human wrecks all skin and bone'. In some areas the railways, roads and bridges had been completely washed away and Marianne was unable to continue with what Lear called her 'Nyngien Toor'. The cold was always her enemy and on several occasions she was forced to take 'her old rheumatic bones down the hill' for fear of a return of the Japanese rheumatism.

Soon after her arrival in India, Marianne made her way to Thanjavur to stay with Dr Burnell, a judge and eminent Sanskrit scholar. Her letter of introduction from Edward Lear described her as 'a great draughtsman and Botanist and altogetheraciously clever and delightful'. She had in fact already met Arthur Burnell on the boat going to Java and had formed an immediate respect for him when he had contradicted her for saying that *Amherstia nobilis* was a sacred plant, something which Sir William Hooker had told her. Dr Burnell had said that Sir William had been a great botanist but was no Hindu scholar. (The plant is however sacred to Burmese Buddhists.) He himself was engaged in writing a book about the sacred plants of the Hindus, and Marianne then determined to illustrate his work. The fortnight with Dr Burnell was memorable and soon Marianne was writing with great affection, 'if you are so much to me in so short a time, you must be infinitely more to those who have known you longer ... There thems my sentiments'. Arthur Burnell was never strong and was to die in San Remo in 1882, when he was in his very early forties. She once wrote offering to nurse him should he get ill: 'send for me and I will come and nurse you and shock the world of old women as I did at Netley with Dudley [her cousin] – what a contrast you two would be. He the most prejudiced and orthodox of unthinking soldiers and you a bohemian like myself ...' She confided to him of the terrible void

Nepalese temple and peepul or bo tree, *Ficus religiosa*, with blue pigeons bathing.
Varanasi (Benares), India. Edward Lear painted a similar view in 1873.

Rhododendron arboreum ssp *nilagiricum*, native to
south-west India.

The sacred lotus, *Nelumbo nucifera*, 'the most beautiful and graceful of all the
waterlilies'.

African baobab or upside-down-tree, *Adansonia digitata*, in the Princess's
garden at Thanjavur, South India.

Hydrangea anomala and *Thunbergia lutea* painted in Darjeeling.

OPPOSITE LEFT: Foliage, flowers and fruit of the African sausage tree, *Kigelia africana*, which Marianne painted by candlelight in India. The flowers are pollinated by bats and are described variously as smelling of fox, fish, cucumber, sour milk and mouse!

OPPOSITE RIGHT: View from Rungaroon, near Darjeeling, India, with a tree in the foreground covered with epiphytes.

Often she worked for twelve hours a day, frequently getting soaked in the process. Her attempts were sometimes hindered by ants who seemed to have an especial taste for both Marianne and her oil paints, or by the black crows who stole her tubes of paint. In all she completed about two hundred paintings during her fifteen-month stay.

By 21 March 1879 Marianne was back in cold and icy England. Friends flocked round to her flat in Victoria Street eager to hear about India and admire her latest sketches. It was all very wearisome telling the same stories time and time again, so she decided to hire a room in a gallery in Conduit Street to exhibit her 'oil sketches of India and the Archipelago painted on the spot'. The exhibition was open for two months and *The Studio* described it as 'intelligent and useful applied art labour'.

After the exhibition was over, Marianne went to visit her sister and brother-in-law at Davos in Switzerland but the cold 'did not agree with my old body' and so she went on to Italy. Here she was delighted to see Edward Lear, who uncorked all kinds of nonsense for her benefit. He would stop in the busy streets to deliver each joke, so that Marianne thought the Italians must wonder who the old pair of lunatics were. His laughing doses did her more good than any doctor's physic. At his villa in San Remo he made her eat 'pellucid periwinkle soup, mulberry jam, and every other luxury only Mr Lear could think of'. One wonders if it was served with a runcible spoon.

Returning home again, she was thrilled that her offer of pictures and a gallery at Kew had been accepted by Sir Joseph Hooker. A further excitement was an invitation from Charles Darwin, who had expressed a wish to meet the remarkable Miss North. He told

her that she should not attempt any representation of the world's flora without seeing the peculiar vegetation of Australia. She felt this was a 'royal command' and decided to go at once.

Australia

The voyage to Australia (via Sarawak and the Brookes) was full of interest and, as the ship neared the new continent, she was warned by a curious woman-hating Russian baron, that the Brisbane hotel she planned to stay in was 'the most hateful hole in the universe ... beastly food and rooms ... but would do for a lady'. Marianne did not stay long, as she received an invitation from Government House, whose garden opened straight into the Botanic Garden. However, she found the city unattractive, the gardens dried up, the hospitality of the old-fashioned order and the araucarias not a patch on those in the Temperate House at Kew.

Rhododendrons of North India. Above, *Rhododendron dalhousiae* painted from a plant growing in a glasshouse at Jackman's Nursery at Kingston, and below, *Rhododendron maddenii* ssp *maddenii* pictured from a plant in those gardens.

LEFT: The giant waterlily, *Victoria amazonica*. Painted during a foggy winter in London, the painting was based on 'W. Fitch's splendid illustration and aided by the memory of its magnificence in tropical gardens'.

Scene in a West Australian forest. Large trees of black butt and red gum, *Eucalyptus calophylla*, with undergrowth of grass trees, *Xanthorrhoea, Banksia, Kingia*, the cycad, *Macrozamia riedlei*, with fine old specimens of *Kingia australis* in the foreground.

Flowers of the waratah,
Telopea speciosissima, from the
Blue Mountains,
New South Wales.

West Australian vegetation: jarrah, *Eucalyptus marginata*, with the handsome red-flowered *Grevillea banksii* and a galah or cockatoo, *Eulophus roseicapillus*.

Flower-spikes of *Banksia attenuata* from Western Australia, in various stages of development.

Wildflowers of Albany, West Australia. In the foreground, among others, are: *Anthocercis viscosa*, the large white flower; *Thysanotus* species, purple flowers with fringed petals; *Leschenaultia biloba*, deep blue flowers; behind is *Burtonia conferta*. Hanging in front of the base are *Kennedya coccinea*, with the elegant blue *Sollya fusiformis* on the right and the white and pale-pink inflorescence above, somewhat like a Maltese cross, is *Xanthosia rotundifolia*, intermixed with *Pimelea rosea*. Above these is a species of *Petrophila*, with the pink, hop-like inflorescence of *Johnsonia lupulina*. Behind and to the right are several species of *Stylidium*, with a dark purple-brown *Tetratheca filiformis* in front.

'Possum up a gum tree',
Australia.

Kangaroos hopping down a hillside in Queensland with a background of
bunya-bunya pines, *Araucaria bidwillii*.

Soon all this was left behind as she started on her great antipodean exploration. At every turn she came across new plants which needed their portraits painting – extraordinary forests of eucalyptus or gum trees, wattles or acacias with their yellow balls of flowers, banksias, dripping with delicious honey, tree ferns and many other things she had never even dreamed of. The vegetation of Western Australia was unbelievably rich, like a natural flower garden – without moving she could pick twenty-five different flowers. She was fascinated too by the birds and animals – brilliantly coloured parrots, black swans, huge pelicans, laughing jackasses, and hundreds of cockatoos who flew ahead of them screeching and then 'settling on a tree for a gossip' before flying on again. There were koalas, shy platypuses, mice with fringed tails who seemed to glide through the air like bats and, in the Bunya Mountains, she had her first sight of a party of kangaroos hopping down a hillside in a comical procession. The Australian people were very friendly and Marianne particularly approved of the women, who were indepen-dent, efficient and sensible.

She visited all sorts of out-of-the-way places, sometimes travelling into the bush where trees and bushes had to be chopped down to enable the buggy to proceed. In Sydney she visited the Botanic Garden but lamented the new houses which were springing up like fungi all round the town. Melbourne she thought a noble city and it was there that she met the great German botanist, Baron von Mueller, who was much excited by her painting of the rare *Eucalyptus macrocarpus* and when she showed him a bud which she was saving for Kew, he calmly pocketed it with 'Fair Lady, you permit I take that'.

In Albany, Western Australia, Marianne stayed with Ellis Rowan (1848–1922) the brilliant Australian botanical and wildlife artist, who had that year won a gold medal for her wildflower paintings at the Melbourne International Exhibition. Marianne thought Mrs Rowan 'a very pretty fairy-like little woman, always well-dressed ...' and much admired her exquisite and delicate watercolours done 'in a peculiar way of her own on gray [sic] paper'. In a letter to Sir Joseph Hooker, Marianne described Mrs Rowan's pictures as 'very beautiful and worth your attention'. It is believed that Marianne may have given Mrs Rowan tuition in oil painting, for although the

A natural fernery in Victoria.

Flowers and seed-vessels of
the West Australian gum tree,
Eucalyptus ficifolia,
with honeysuckers.

View from Collaroy, New South Wales, looking towards the Liverpool Downs. The plain is dotted with gum trees and the river bordered by casuarinas, with red-winged parrots, *Aprosmictus erythropterus*, perching in the branches of the peppermint tree, *Eucalyptus piperita*, in the foreground.

Wildflowers of the Blue Mountains, New South Wales. Conspicuous in this collection is the star-like inflorescence of the flannelflower, *Actinotus helianthi*, while lying in the left foreground is a dark blue *Patersonia* and a rose-flowered *Boronia*. Other species represented belong to the genera *Pimelea, Diuris, Eriostemon, Epacris, Correa, Kennedya, Daviesia, Helichrysum, Lambertia, Styphelia* and *Tetratheca*.

Evening glow over 'The Range', seen through red gums
at Harlaxton, Queensland.

West Australian vegetation. Flowers and fruits of *Banksia coccinea*, with the flowers of the climbing *Gompholobium polymorphum*, with a distant view of King George's Sound.

The bottle tree, *Brachychiton rupestris*, of Queensland, with a grass fire beyond, through which Marianne and her companions had to gallop.

Australian artist continued painting her 'botanical bunches' in watercolour, it was after this visit that she began to experiment in oils; indeed at the Centennial International Exhibition in Melbourne in 1888, Mrs Rowan's prizewinning exhibit was a large painting of chrysanthemums done in oils. It is probable too that Ellis Rowan was inspired by the intrepid Englishwoman's account of her astonishing travels, for in 1883 she took the first of her long and arduous journeys to paint the plants and wildlife of other lands.

Most of the Australians had extraordinarily healthy appetites. Prodigious quantities of beef were served in both houses and inns. At one hostelry there were beefsteaks for breakfast, roast beef for dinner and boiled beef for tea. Cobbe & Co, a firm whose coaches served all Australia, were much excited by transporting Marianne and a lady friend (the first ladies who had apparently travelled by their firm's coaches) and wired for extra beef to be available at their next stopping place. Marianne enjoyed dipping her cup into the billy, the huge saucepan in which the tea was boiled, and once, when they were trying to boil the billy, the surrounding vegetation caught fire and they all had to flee.

Tasmania and New Zealand

Tasmania was not a success, being too much like England. The weather was English as well – drizzling rain and cold, so Marianne felt reluctant to explore. She felt good for nothing, with a gum-boil and a swollen face, but was not allowed to rest. The only thing which redeemed Tasmania was the opossum mice and she persuaded an old barber to part with three of these creatures. The old man was very reluctant to give up his big-eared soft balls of fluff and almost cried at the parting. The mice travelled with Marianne to New Zealand, and because of the cold 'Mr and Mrs Henry' and their daughter were sent on ahead with human friends to Wellington, where it was warmer.

New Zealand was no better and Marianne had some hard words to say about it. There *were* interesting plants, such as the extraordinary sheep plant (*Raoulia*), which even shepherds sometimes mistook for members of their flock, but the weather was cold and the railways were crowded with objectionable children. The views she had heard of she never saw and she found the scenery bare and savage. She had an attack of diarrhoea and her bones

Australian sandalwood, *Santalum spicatum*, and opossum mouse, painted in Western Australia.

Group of nikau palms, *Rhopalostylis sapida*, with background of kawa-kawa, *Piper excelsum*, New Zealand.

Blue African lily, *Agapanthus* species, with large swallow-tail butterfly, *Papilio orphidicephalus*, Natal.

began to ache with rheumatism; another gum-boil appeared and soon she was sick of everything belonging to that cold, heartless island and longed to be home without having the trouble of getting there. The Wellington Botanic Garden was lovely but the people were dreary and the only piece of unspoilt natural bush was strewn with litter, sandwich papers and ginger beer bottles. For once she was only too pleased to rest at Government House and was delighted to hear the Governor abuse the country with as much heartiness as she did.

Marianne returned to England by way of Honolulu and America in company with her mice and the next year was spent organizing the Gallery at Kew. After the opening of the Gallery there was no question of staying quietly at home. The lure of the tropics and the promise of new plants was too strong. 'All the continents of the world had some sort of representation in my Gallery except Africa, and I resolved to begin painting there without loss of time.'

South Africa

By the end of August 1882 Marianne was in Cape Town and for the next nine months she travelled extensively round South Africa. The wealth and brilliance of the flowers staggered her and reminded her of Western Australia. There were quantities of gladioli, heaths, salvias and lobelias, marvellous gazanias 'turning their eyes to the sun', mesembryanthemums, clumps of agapanthus, and innumerable other treasures. It was the proteas however that impressed her most. 'They take me by storm. I never had an idea of them and their variety.' People brought her armfuls of flowers, so many that she did not know what to paint first. Everyone was extraordinarily interested in her painting. One woman asked whether they were 'hand work' or whether she used a machine, another remarked 'She

OPPOSITE: A medley of flowers from the Table Mountain, Cape of Good Hope. On the right, the scarlet *Sutherlandia frutescens* with white ball-like flowers of a *Brunia* and a blue and red *Lobostemon*. Below the *Sutherlandia*, cones and male inflorescence of *Leucodendron platyspermum* with a purple-flowered composite in between. To the left the everlasting *Helipterum speciosissimum*, with white flowers, and a blue *Lobelia*. On the left *Disa cornuta* with dark blue and white hooded flowers and thick leaves mottled red, and *Mimetes cucullatus* with whitish flowers and pink bracts.

An old Dutch vase with South African flowers, painted at Groot Poort. At the top the blue *Moraea tripetala* and two *Moraea bellendenii*. On the right crimson *Antholyza* and next to it on the left is *Gladiolus orchidiflorus*. The large rosy flower with dark blue centre is *Spiloxene capensis*, a yellow *Babiana* hangs on the left and below is the pale yellow *Grielum tenuifolium*. On the right pale yellow *Sparaxis grandiflora* and densely crowded *Ornithogalum thrysoides*.

Wildflowers of Ceres, South Africa. In the centre the yellow 'tea plant', *Rafnia amplexicaulis*, whose leaves are used to make a tea often mixed with ordinary tea. The heath above on the right is *Erica grandiflora*, with a *Mesembryanthemum*, a *Watsonia* and a *Gladiolus* below; there is a white *Moraea* at the top and below on the left. In front *Leucospermum cordifolium*, a species of *Protea* on the left, and white and pink varieties of *Cyphia volubilis* hanging from the vase.

South African sundews (*Drosera*) and other flowers. Above, a plant of the beautiful *Monsonia speciosa* with *Babiana*(?) *rubrocyanea* and *Homeria miniata* on the left, with *Drosera cistiflora* with white flowers, and *D pauciflora* with pale-purple flowers.

Honeyflowers, *Protea repens*, and malachite sunbirds, *Nectarinia famosa*, entwined by *Microloma tenuifolium*, South Africa.

Flowers of St John's. Beginning on the right at the top there is a dark blue *Coleotrype natalensis*, a purplish-red balsam, *Impatiens* species, clusters of the small white flowers of the white pear, *Apodytes dimidiata*, the red and black seed-vessels of which lie at the foot of the basket on the right, and a *Loranthus* with reddish flowers. In the centre is a white *Pavetta*, with immediately over it the purple-red flowers of *Vigna vexillata* and a solitary flower of the yellow *Sphedamnocarpus pruriens*. Returning to the right are two pale-orange flowers and narrow-tendrilled leaves of *Littonia modesta*, a single lily, followed by the more showy deeper-orange *Crocosmia aurea*, a large *Hibiscus* with purple centre, the purplish *Grewia lasiocarpa*, with an *Ipomoea* below. Lying in front is a branch of *Acridocarpus natalitius*.

'"Coming out" of a Cape beauty', painted at Miss Duckett's farm at Groot Poort, South Africa. One of the ostriches turned its head from side to side to listen to voices while still half-enclosed in the shell.

just takes a flower and does it all at once in colours'. Then there were the tiresome girls who crowded into Marianne's room and sorely tried her patience with idiotic questions: wasn't she afraid of spoiling her eyes – shouldn't she save them? Save them for what? Marianne lost her temper and they fled from the room. 'They thought me mad' she recorded, with some satisfaction.

Marianne spent some time staying with a Miss Duckett, a commanding woman, who ran a large farm at Groot Poort. The fifty ostriches who stalked round the farm were a great source of amusement, but the abundance of fleas there did not make it so desirable. At Cadles she at last managed to paint *Protea cynaroides*, the biggest of all the proteas, sometimes known as the king protea. Ever since her arrival she had been seeking a specimen in full flower and when at last the prize was brought to her, she almost cried with joy! 'The bracts were like pink satin, tinted at the base with green,

and a perfect pyramid of yellow flowers rose in the centre.' At Verulam she met an enthusiastic botanist who took her to see some rare aloes, which were the sole remains of a great forest. He told her that Kew 'had coolly asked him to cut one down and send them a "section" for the museum!'

Marianne was fascinated by all the native people: the Zulu men and women whom she saw harvesting the cotton; the Pondo natives with fish and bird bones stuck through their ears and their hair stiffened with grease and glue; and the Kaffirs dressed in their red drapery and feathers, who stalked through the bush with superb dignity. However, by the end of May she was feeling ill and homesick and deafness was beginning to trouble her. She had worked without cease and by the time she returned home she had completed over one hundred paintings. Nevertheless, a few months later, she was off again, this time to the Seychelles.

Looking upstream from the mouth of the St John's River, Kaffraria. Various
aloes, *Strelitzia alba* and mesembryanthemums may be seen on the rocks
in front.

Amatungula, *Carissa macrocarpa*, in flower and fruit, and blue ipomoea, *Ipomoea lapathifolia*, painted at the mouth of the Kowie River, South Africa.

Angraecum sesquipedale and *Urania* moths of Madagascar, painted in South Africa. The orchid has the longest spur of any known orchid and Darwin predicted it would be pollinated by a moth with a very long proboscis; this was afterwards confirmed by the discovery of the moth, *Xanthopan morgani praedicta.*

Vegetation of the Addo Bush with Kaffirs and their habitations. The nests hanging from the trees are those of a 'social finch'. On the right a species of *Aloe* and the trees with purplish flowers are *Portulacaria afra*, the spekboom.

Aloes at Natal. Marianne was much impressed by these plants, with their red-hot-poker flowers.

OPPOSITE: 'Social birds and social herbs' at Malmesbury, South Africa: *Zantedeschia aethiopica* with great reed mace, *Typha capensis*, hung with nests of social birds, with *Leucospermum conocarpodendron* ssp *conocarpodendron*, the krippelboom, on the right.

Water-loving plants and a kingfisher, near Grahamstown, South Africa. Floating in the water is *Nymphoides thunbergiana*; in front are two varieties of *Eucomis comosa*, with the orchid, *Disa racemosa*, and a species of *Cyperus* behind.

Ipomoea palmata, a common plant of the tropics, and vavangue, *Vangueria edulis*, with Mahé harbour, Seychelles, in the distance. The vavangue is a native of Madagascar, but now cultivated in other countries for its edible fruit.

Female coco de mer, *Lodoicea maldivica*, with fruit covered with small green lizards, Seychelles.

The Madagascar periwinkle, *Catharanthus roseus*, and green frogs. Today this plant is valued for its use in the treatment of cancer.

The only shade in Ile Aride, Seychelles, under a partly uprooted tree of *Terminalia catappa*.

Dr and Mrs Hoad's house in Praslin, Seychelles. The hen-coops and roof caps are made of the leaves of the coco de mer and other palms.

Foliage, flowers and fruit of the capucin tree, *Northea seychellana*, named by Sir Joseph Hooker in honour of Marianne. The bird is almost certainly meant to be the Madagascar fody, *Foudia madagascariensis*; it should have a black beak however.

OPPOSITE: A study of fruit grown in the Seychelles: raspberries, *Rubus rosifolius*, in the banana-leaf 'boat', with mango, *Mangifera indica*, and soursop, *Annona muricata*, and seed of the capucin tree, *Northea seychellana*, in the foreground.

arms of an octopus. I have seen the thing and mean to like it'. The mangoes were as good as any she had tasted and the wild raspberries, brought down from the hills in baskets made of banana leaves, were delicious stewed and served with cream. Of the many islands she visited, Praslin was 'the most perfect situation I ever was in'. She delighted in paddling 'without shoes and stockings' but 'pinna shells and corals are like knives and spoil the fun rather'. It was while in the Seychelles that she made a study of a tree which afterwards was declared by Sir Joseph Hooker to be a new genus and named *Northea sechellana*, after Marianne.

Then Marianne's health began to break down seriously. All those months and years of travelling, often getting soaked through and sometimes not eating properly, had taken their toll. She was fifty-three years of age, her rheumatism was getting worse, her deafness increasing, and her 'nerves', or what has been described as a sort of paranoid condition, were causing her to hear voices. Because of some deaths from smallpox, she was unable to return home and agreed to go into quarantine on Long Island with some other passengers. Here she became very disturbed and began to imagine all sorts of tricks being played on her. People seemed to be mocking her and screaming with laughter. She thought they let rats loose in her room and, believing people were going to rob or murder her, barricaded herself in and stitched all her money into her clothes. It was a nightmare and one she never forgot.

Eventually she was back in England trying to forget those terrible days which, strangely, she half realized were some sort of delusion. She busied herself at Kew arranging her paintings in the new room which had been built at the back of the Gallery. It was in August that a great pleasure came to her in the form of a letter from Queen Victoria, written by her Private Secretary, Sir Henry Ponsonby. The Queen regretted that there was no way of publicly acknowledging Miss North's great gift to the nation but asked her to accept a signed photograph of Her Majesty as a token of her esteem and recognition of Marianne's generosity.

There was one more journey to be undertaken. Much against the advice of her family and friends Marianne set off in August 1884 for Chile, determined to paint both *Araucaria araucana*, the 'Puzzle-monkey tree' and the great blue *Puya alpestris*.

Male inflorescence and ripe nuts of the coco de mer, *Lodoicea maldivica*, Seychelles.

Chile

In Chile, tiresomely, people told her there were no specimens of the *Puya* in flower, others declared they did not exist. With her usual determination however Marianne soon located specimens and a man in Santiago was bribed to bring her one. It was a poor example, almost as wretched as the one she had tried to draw in the Cactus House at Kew, but it was still exciting. She decided that an expedition must be made with a guide and a horse to its native habitat in the Cordilleras Mountains.

At times in the mountains, when it became too steep, they had to dismount and proceed on foot through thick clouds. Nothing could be seen but Marianne would not give up. Eventually the mists cleared and she was rewarded with the sight of 'a great group of noble flowers, standing like ghosts at first and then coming out with their full beauty of colour and form in every stage of growth; while beyond them glittered a snow peak far away'. There was blue sky overhead too. It was yet another new world of wonders.

There were the same difficulties in trying to find the monkey puzzle tree. People said the forests were difficult to reach, that they were dangerous and she might be carried off by the Indians or even eaten by pumas. Others declared the trees had been chopped down and used for railway sleepers. However a two-hour rail journey (she had been given a free pass on all the railways by the Government of Chile) took her to Angol and a further four- to five-hour ride with an Irish gentleman, who owned the forests, brought her within sight of her goal. The trees looked 'like pins loosely stuck into pincushions as they stood out black against the sunset sky' and soon she was settling down to paint her latest portrait.

Sadly, by the end of her visit to Chile, Marianne was feeling wretched and ill – her nerves 'were following her everywhere'. In Lima she consulted an old German doctor who gave her 'bromide', which had 'as much effect as toast and water', and decided to return home, via Jamaica, where she rested with an old friend and was prescribed yet more useless 'bromide'.

Chilean flowers in twin maté pot, and strawberries. In the background *Fabiana imbricata* and a species of *Tigridia*, deep blue *Pasithea caerulea*, yellow *Mimulus luteus*, pink *Centaurium quitense*, a small *Centaurea*, fruit of *Aristotelia chilensis* and flowerhead of *Senecio*(?); in front a branch of *Crinodendron patagua*.

Flowering spike of the blue puya, *Puya alpestris*. One of the objects of Marianne's visit to Chile was to paint this magnificent plant.

OPPOSITE: Wildflowers of Chanleon, Chile. *Fuchsia magellanica* var *macrostema*, on the right, is the wild parent of the hardy cultivated varieties. Above it is the blue *Puya*, with orange anthers, and the orange balls of *Buddleia globosa*, a pale-purple lupin, a yellow-flowered *Chloraea* and crimson *Ourisia coccinea*. Immediately below the last, the orange heads of a species of *Boopis*(?), succeeded by a rosy *Mutisia*(?) *decurrens* and the white-flowered winter's bark, *Drimys winteri*. Lying on the table are the purple-brown *Bomarea salsilla*, a lilac and yellow *Solanum*, the pure white *Libertia ixioides* and *Pernettya mucronata*. The greenish-white pea-flower is *Lathyrus pubescens*. The leaves of *Buddleia globosa* are used as a universal remedy in Chile for the treatment of wounds and sores.

Climbing plants of Chile. The passion flower, *Passiflora pinnatistipula* (above), and *Lardizabala biternata* (below) with dull-purple flowers and edible fruits.

Forest of monkey puzzle trees, *Araucaria araucana*, with seven snowy peaks of
the Cordilleras behind; in the foreground the Chilean fire bush, *Embothrium coccineum*,
an orange-flowerd *Chloraea* species and white-flowered *Libertia ixioides*.

THE OPENING OF THE GALLERY

It took a year between Marianne's trips to Australia and South Africa to prepare the Gallery, patching, sorting, framing and fitting the paintings. She arranged for a dado of exotic woods to be put below the pictures and she herself decorated the doors and their surrounds. As refreshment was not allowed to be served, she painted coffee over one doorway and tea over another. It was all very tiring and by evening she was dead beat and good for nothing.

At last everything was ready and on 7 June 1882, a large concourse of distinguished people from the artistic, scientific, literary and fashionable world attended the Private View. *The Times* reported that the Gallery 'combines in an almost unprecedented degree the qualities of the enthusiastic traveller and accomplished artist'. The *Gardener's Chronicle* described her paintings as 'the skilful dashing works of a true artist, which completely succeed in showing Nature as she is' but remarked, 'we are not quite pleased with the heavy classical ornament under the cornice, and we think the shiny black frames are too strong in colour'. The prismatic tints in her double rainbow over Niagara were queried, but it was suggested that 'a touch of Miss North's admirable and prolific brush' would soon set this right. Marianne was in fact somewhat unconventional in her method of painting. Her sister Catherine said she was intolerant of 'rules', especially in art, and painted as a clever child would. A rough sketch in pen and ink was first made on to the cardboard and then she would apply the colours, squeezed straight from the metal tubes, employing virtually no medium.

The Gallery was regarded as 'one of the most successful picture galleries as regards light in the kingdom'. Fergusson, the designer,

ROYAL GARDENS . KEW.

Picture Gallery erected at the expense of Miss North .

From designs by James Fergusson . F.R.S

had written an essay on the way light was introduced to Greek temples and had put his theories into practice in the North Gallery. Later the *Gardener's Chronicle* stated that it 'could imagine no more valuable adjunct to the unrivalled collections of living and dried plants at Kew'. Sir Joseph Hooker stressed the importance of the paintings as an historical record, particularly as many of the plants 'are already disappearing or are doomed shortly to disappear before the axe and the forest fire, the plough and the flock, of the ever-advancing settler or colonist'. Words today which are sadly even more relevant.

This picture of the Marianne North Gallery appeared in the *Building News* of 15 April 1881. The porch was added later at Marianne North's expense to give shelter to a custodian in charge of 'wet umbrellas and ladies' clogs'.

OPPOSITE: One of the doors from the North Gallery; Marianne herself decorated the surrounds and panels of all the doors in the Gallery.

Mount House, Alderley, Gloucestershire, painted by Marianne,
where she spent her last years.

LAST YEARS

Marianne spent another year after her return from Chile adding new pictures to the Gallery and renumbering the pictures so that all the countries were together. Her strength had gone and she no longer had the desire to visit the once longed-for tropics. She determined to find a quiet country place with a garden where she could end her days 'far from the madding crowd of callers and lawn tennis'.

In the summer of 1886 she found the exact place – a charming old stone house with a garden, fields and an orchard, situated in Alderley, a remote village hidden in the folds of the Cotswolds in Gloucestershire. There, she set about making the 'most perfect garden in England', which she stocked with plants from many parts of the world. Everyone provided her with specimens; Kew sent her all kinds of unusual plants, her nieces brought alpines from Switzerland, and others, such as Gertrude Jekyll and Canon Ellacombe, gave her contributions from their own gardens. Marianne found a sundial in a neighbouring garden and put it up as a monument to Mr Henry, the last survivor of her opossum mice, who was buried underneath. John Addington Symonds wrote an epitaph to this well-travelled mouse, which can still be seen today on a brass plate attached to the sundial.

Even though Marianne had travelled the world and seen the most diverse and exotic vegetation, she was still able to write 'No life is so charming as a country one in England, and no flowers are sweeter or more lovely than the primroses, cowslips, bluebells, and violets which grow in abundance all round me here'.

She gardened when she had the strength and sat writing her memoirs – *Recollections of a Happy Life* she called them – compiled from journals and letters to friends. It was something she had been working on for some years. In 1875 while suffering from a heavy cold, she wrote to the watercolourist, Barbara Bodichon (1827–1891), 'I am a damp unwholesome body, disagreeable to myself and friends, but mean to crush the demon and meanwhile sit by the fire and scribble about warmer places', and in 1877 she informed Dr Burnell of her 'scribbling' remarking 'It is most amusing work even if it never comes to anything more'. It did of course, being edited by her sister Catherine and published after her death.

In her last years Marianne was increasingly isolated by her deafness and tormented by her 'nerves' – those mocking voices, which never ceased. In 1888 liver disease showed itself and she was thought to be dying. She rallied and, strangely, as the disease progressed, her tormentors left her. By the summer of 1890 she was getting no stronger, bleeding came on if she walked and turtle soup did no good. In 1889 she had written 'I merely exist from one operation to another and may cease existence any day. I do not dread it'. She never had feared death, whether under the heels of a horse in Java, shooting the rapids in fragile canoes in Sarawak or cracking her skull against a wall in Japan. On 30 August 1890 Marianne died and was buried in the quiet country churchyard at Alderley, aged only fifty-nine years.

It is at Kew however that she is best remembered. Professor Mangham wrote that 'a visit to this Gallery brings home as perhaps nothing else can in a short while the astonishing array of beautifully coloured forms exhibited by the ever changing mantle of the earth'.

A photograph of Marianne at Alderley, taken in 1887, by a neighbour. Inscribed in Marianne's hand underneath the picture is 'Marianne North at home. Mount House, Alderley. May to November as long as life lasts'.

Although opinions may differ on the merits of Marianne's paintings, what is quite certain is that her Gallery is unique. There is simply nothing like it anywhere in the world. As Wilfrid Blunt once wrote 'The North Gallery is not so much a museum as a museum-piece: something as whimsical, as extraordinary, as "period" and as precious as the Albert Memorial or the Watts Mortuary Chapel at Compton, and it must never, *never* be touched'. Happily 'Aunt Pop's' Gallery remains virtually unchanged and, even today with easy travel and colour photography, it still excites and brightens the day of many a visitor to Kew.

A bust of Marianne sculpted by Conrad Dressler (1856–1940) in 1893, based on photographs and other memorabilia, in the North Gallery at Kew. Dressler found the commission a very difficult one owing to the contradictory nature of the documents and the widely divergent opinions of the visitors. The bust was presented to Kew by Marianne's sister, Catherine, in 1894.

INDEX

Page numbers in *italics* denote illustrations.